Foreword

For many years the collaboration of NSEAD and Berol Ltd., through the annual award of a bursary, has resulted in the support of various forms of curriculum development in art, craft and design. Occasionally this has led to the publication of a text, the product of the award holder. It is gratifying that one of the latest winners of the bursary, David Nicholls, has produced such an inspiring record of the use of computers in art and design, by children with physical disabilities. When interviewed for the bursary, David stated that his aim was publication because he felt that the work of the Thurlow Park School students deserved a wider audience. This book has fulfilled that aim: but I believe it has gone beyond mere exposure of computer images.

The presentation avoids jargon and sets the students' products in the context of a compassionate educational experience. It is refreshing to find familiar art and design terms applied to the methodology. David refers to 'observation' in establishing the main elements of a picture, to a student being visibly and contageously excited as the 'connections' were made and the 'ideas' poured out. Underpinning the activity is David's personal philosophy which surfaces at appropriate places throughout the text.

David's whole approach is that of the creative practitioner. This is not an instruction manual for the generation of computer images on prescribed equipment using identified painting packages. It is a celebration of the creative art work of students who would have found the manipulation of conventional art materials difficult and discouraging. The illustrations demonstrate the extent of their independent inventiveness. This is possible because David consciously seeks to aviod imposing too many external controls on the students while developing their self-trust and confidence. At a time of expensive attempts at imposing massive external control, here is wonderful evidence of the success, in art and design, of 'giving a push to let go'.

Michael Yeomans
President, NSEAD
1994-1995

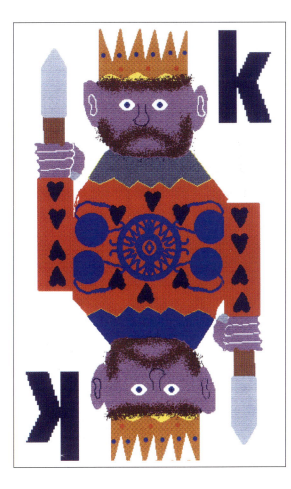

KING

by Stephen Saddler
(Thurlow Park School)
extended page 320 x
512 pixels

This celebration of the artists of Thurlow Park School is dedicated to
Ricardo Caballero
10 November 1976–15 October 1995

POOLING IDEAS

ON ART AND IMAGING

DAVID NICHOLLS

Trentham Books and NSEAD

NSEAD
NATIONAL SOCIETY FOR EDUCATION IN ART & DESIGN

With funding from the Arts Council of England

First published in 1997 by Trentham Books Limited in association with
the National Society for Education in Art and Design
With funding from the Arts Council of England.

Trentham Books Limited
Westview House
734 London Road
Oakhill
Stoke-on-Trent
Staffordshire
England ST4 5NP

British Cataloguing in Publication Data
A catalogue record for this book is available from the British Library.

ISBN: 185856 059 4

Designed and typeset by Trentham Print Design, Chester and printed by
Qualitex Printing Limited, Cardiff

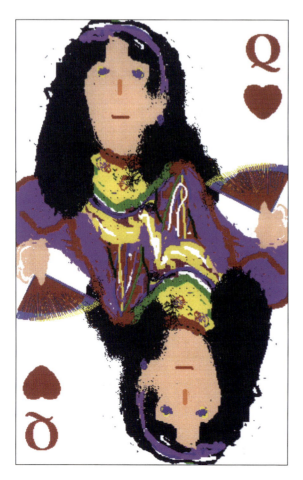

QUEEN

by Mary Cameron

(Clapham Park School)

extended page 320 x

512 pixels

Introduction

Thurlow Park is an all-age school for children with physical disabilities. Since 1978 I have taught art throughout the school from nursery to school leaving age. The art room provides a rich environment where the pupils enjoy the sensory stimulus of paint and clay and many other materials. The room is also equipped with tools and machinery for shaping wood and plastic and there is a pottery kiln. It is important for all children to experience an environment rich in colour and texture but it is absolutely essential for those with physical disabilities. By enriching the material surroundings we thus increase the opportunities for augmenting sensory input.

In 1988 computers were introduced into the art curriculum to allow us to experiment with image manipulation and animation.[1] It was felt that image manipulation and the resulting printed pictures would enhance exhibitions for examination purposes. And indeed, as expected, this has proved to be the case – but in unexpected ways. I also thought that animation might be fun to do with the younger children, and so it is, but it has proved also to be a useful tool in the development of picture making skills.

The machines we used first were some borrowed RM Nimbus PC 186s with Paintspa and Art+Time software. Prints were produced on an Integrex Colourjet printer. Funding was applied for to buy our own equipment and, in the interim, between applying for funding and receiving it, I embarked upon my own research project, visiting colleges and software writers and dealers and computer shows. When funding was finally agreed, initially from BBC Children In Need and Sir John Cass's Foundation[2], I opted for the Commodore AMIGA and Deluxe Paint software. Other image manipulation packages were bought and tried, but none proved as satisfying as Deluxe Paint. Simple page turning animation is possible in Deluxe Paint, and this is sometimes built into the problems set for the senior students. Another animation program

sometimes used is Fantavision, which is not as direct to use as Deluxe Paint but incorporates tweening to produce smooth movement. Also it has a bank of simple sound effects that can be easily added to the animation, frame by frame.

An HP PaintJet printer was acquired at the same time as the AMIGAs. The machine uses continuous sheet (Z fold) paper and this, in combination with the posters function in Deluxe Photolab software, makes large prints easy to produce.

The first GCSE Art & Design (unendorsed) exhibition, incorporating prints from the work using computers, was a turning point in the way art was to be delivered to the senior students. The Midland Examining Group moderators felt that the exhibitions were enhanced by the work that had been created using computers and so the final grades awarded were slightly higher than they would have been without the prints. But the moderators also felt that the other more conventional works, painting and drawing and ceramics, were detracting from the high quality of the prints. The solution they suggested was, to change the examination offer to Art & Design, endorsed Graphics. So long as there was sufficient variety of approach and subject matter this could all be produced using painting programs.

I assumed that this difference in quality was due simply to lack of finish. Art work in conventional materials inevitably reflects the hand of the artist. Physical weakness can show as weakness in handling of materials. Involuntary muscular spasm, though expressive as gesture, can also be destructive, punching holes in paper with pencil or brush, or simply leaving the paper creased untidily after it has come adrift from its fixings and folded under physical onslaught. The colour print from a painting program has clarity and freshness but is also, in a sense, unfinished, for a print often stimulates the student to further exploration, adjusting the colour or tightening the composition.

WILLOW

by Owen Attard

(extended page 320 x
333 pixels)

From 1988 to 1994 the GCSE Art & Design group
was joined by students with visual impairment from
Clapham Park School. They also gained enormously
from being able to work on computers.

The examination results for all the students
showed an immediate improvement, and grades A
and B are now the norm. And it would seem to be
the result of a fairly simple equation, viz., top
quality image manipulation software plus good
quality printer using best quality paper results in
high quality final product for good examination
results. The reality, however, is somewhat more
complex.

A good image manipulation program establishes
confidence and, through confidence, self-esteem,
self-belief. They feed and grow upon each other,
and with them grows a feeling of security. Many of
our students may never have felt that degree of
security before, perhaps not since infancy. It would
be easy at Thurlow Park to find reasons for this:
loss of strength and loss of control through
increasing disability, or loss of self-confidence
through increasing awareness of disability. The

students become more experimental, more playful.
But this increase in confidence could be equally
true for mainstream students with no apparent
motor problems.

At Thurlow Park School the work on computers
grew out of, and is structured in relation to,
established practices of painting, drawing, collage,
etc. Photography was also used and sculptural
forms were made in resistant materials such as
foamboard, ceramics, and vacuum-formed plastic –
materials and processes that would not be out of
place in an art college situation but which, in many
secondary schools, have been appropriated by
technology. All the work illustrated here has been
produced by students engaged in their own
personal, sometimes intense, exploration of the
possibilities of this still developing medium. There
is some reference to function but the main purpose
has been to show by example that images
produced on computer using a painting program
need not look machine made. For me, many of the
images are quite magical, displaying both charm and
humour. Knowing the students as well as I do,
some of the images seem miraculous.

Whatever the arguments against using computers
for art and design, it should not be forgotten that,
for people with poor hand control or whose reach
is severely restricted or whose eyesight is
extremely weak, the combination of a good
mousedriven painting program and a bright image
on a monitor screen can seem like heaven.

Pooling Ideas

Tzu-Kung, the disciple of Confucius, after travelling to Ch`u in the south, came back by way of Chin. When he was passing through Han-Yin he saw an old man who was engaged in irrigating his vegetable plots. The way the old man did it was to let himself down into the well-pit by footholes cut in the side and emerge clasping a pitcher which he carefully emptied into a channel, thus expending a great deal of energy with very small results.

'There exists,' Tzu-Kung said to him, 'a contrivance which can irrigate a hundred vegetable plots in a single day. Unlike what you are doing, it demands a very small expenditure of energy, but produces very great results. Would you like me to tell you about it?' The gardener raised his head and gazed at Tzu-Kung 'What is it like?' he asked. 'It is an instrument carved out of wood,' said Tzu-Kung, 'heavy behind and light in front. It scoops up water like a bale, as quickly as one drains a bath-tub. Its name is the well-sweep.' A look of indignation came into the gardener's face. He laughed scornfully, saying, 'I used to be told by my teacher that where there are cunning contrivances there will be cunning performances, and where there are cunning performances there will be cunning hearts. He in whose breast a cunning heart lies has blurred the pristine purity of his nature; he who has blurred the pristine purity of his nature has troubled the quiet of his soul; and with one who has troubled the quiet of his soul Tao will not dwell. It is not that I do not know about this invention, but I should be ashamed to use it.'[3]

Many of us have an ambivalent attitude toward machines. The internal combustion engine is both noisy and noisome but we value the vehicle for the ease and speed with which it can transport us. Not that any of us would seriously object to the well-sweep or shaduf. It helped the Ancient Egyptians sustain their earthly paradise for thousands of years, and Chuang Tzu was really stressing the importance of using things as things, and not allowing ourselves to be used by things as things.

But as with the gardener, so there are those who shrink from contact with computers and painting programs, assuming perhaps that anything done *with* a computer is somehow done *by* the computer.

A painting program, as any medium, can be used with more or less art. It can be used simply as a means for generating repeat patterns or colour variations of existing motifs, or for experimenting with different compositions by rearranging the elements of a picture, or for demonstrating linear perspective. Mechanical processes are executed that might otherwise take time to work through. The painting program is used as an extension of other media, and the computer comes to be regarded as a labour-saving object, perhaps kept locked away in a corner of a studio to be turned to only for fixing specific problems. Just another tool to be used for processes that may be directed remotely by a teacher familiar with the program, like, perhaps, typing from dictation or painting by numbers. And 'just another tool' became, for a time, a kind of slogan, as though to reassure ourselves and others that we were using this new medium in the politically correct way, as an extension of the 'normal' curriculum, and not as a novel and surprising invention that might actually revolutionise and liberate us creatively.

New materials, new technologies, invariably polarise attitudes, engendering both rejection *and* imitation before the general 'invisibility that comes

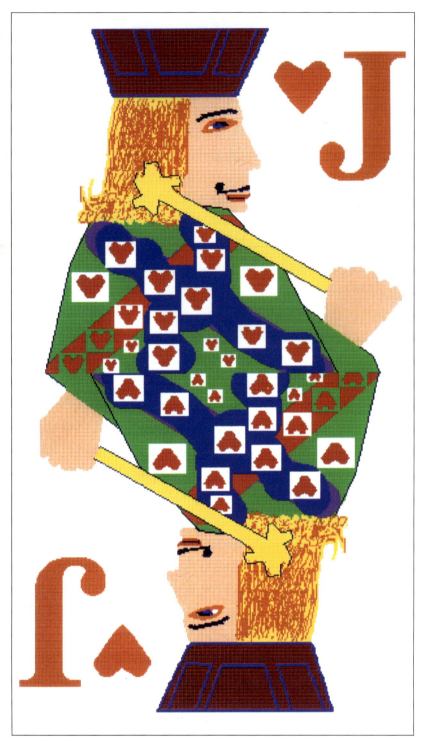

JACK

by Owen Attard

(extended page 320 x 512 pixels)

in time with familiarity'.[4] A separate study could be made tracing this interchange throughout history and beyond, for example, the influence of painting on photography, followed by the influence of photography on painting; timber construction details in cast-iron or stone; the first copper blades hammered into shapes of knapped flint; the finest obsidian blades made in imitation of bronze casting. It is tempting to go on to consider the bee and the bee orchid, or cuckoos and their species-specific eggs, since we do well always to compare natural organic processes. For it is this 'invisibility' that comes with familiarity which can blind us to the value of the unfamiliar, be this from another culture or the new in our own. The unfamiliar seems unnatural even though culture is totally unnatural, which is why its manifestations are all the more remarkable. Wood and egg yolks and lapis lazuli and gold are all natural materials but there is nothing natural about the way they are used in tempera painting, although that is not the reason why it is has been the medium for the creation of images of a supernatural beauty. Linen and linseed oil are reassuringly natural organic products derived from flax but there is nothing natural about the cultural practice of oil painting. Referring to oil painting as a cultural practice seems very odd but it can perhaps help us shift our focus. There is nothing natural about cameras and photography but what is more natural than light? And there is nothing natural about computers but what is more natural than electricity, the stuff of lightning and flashes of inspiration? We need to be aware of the hierarchy of materials and practices for what it is. Creativity, natural or supernatural, is the motor of evolution, of growth, of life. We are all born reaching for the world, physically, emotionally, intellectually, spiritually, and the richness of our world depends upon the richness of the 'language' we have to experience it, the 'language' of our culture, the 'languages' of other cultures. In that sense, the world is our creative construct.

There are many well documented examples of people whose ability to cope with the world on a daily basis is severely restricted but who are able to perform in a gifted way with a musical instrument or a drawing instrument or in the manipulation of numbers, just as there are many artists who have a feeling for one particular medium to the exclusion of all others. So we as teachers have a responsibility to ensure that our own preferences do not blind us to the possibilities of other, perhaps new, 'cultural practices', and that our students are given every opportunity to explore, as fully as they are able, a rich variety of materials. I have taught students who have shown no aptitude with brush or pencil but who came to excel at creating pictures in a painting program because they felt motivated, reassured, secure. But this has required users be given single machines, and the time to get to know the program and the freedom to become immersed, absorbed. By denying our students access to this new medium we could be denying them their only possible language of creative expression.

I once saw some children's drawings of the budding ends of horse chestnut branches. The children had been encouraged to annotate their drawings with observations of texture, colour, stickiness, etc.. They had used hard pencils on thin newsprint paper. For the following session, the teacher had enriched the materials by providing cartridge paper and a range of graded pencils. The children had produced more drawings, but this time their notes all referred to the pencils, for example '2B pencils can make lines this black'. Their attention had shifted to the new equipment.

A similar shift has happened with computers and imaging programs, and for some the shift has stuck. By labelling the product computer art or computer painting or computer graphics we perhaps add the risk of conjuring obvious examples that are merely illustrative of function, where digitised images and special effects have become ends in themselves. The product looks mechanical because it is the result of machine-like processes. It looks and is vacuous because it exists in a vacuum of self-referral.

CITY

by Isaac Williams (Clapham Park School) standard page 320 x 256 pixels

We can perhaps remember learning to read and write, the stumbling-blocks we encountered, the incomprehensibility of the awkward marks, the centrifugal pull on the muscles of our hand and fingers as we struggled to counter the straight line, driving our pencil to make a corner or close a curve. We remember even as we scan, unaware of any threshold between the thought and this once foreign medium which we now own.

In the same way, using a mouse or trackball for the first time can feel odd and awkward. It may even feel disabling of us as fine artists, and it begins to seem absurdly materialistic that this minor art form should require for its production a cumbersome and expensive pile of hardware[5] processor, monitor, keyboard – trackball or mouse or graphics tablet – power – printer. All this can seem, at first, impossibly and ponderously mechanical. But, far from accepting that it is materialistic, I am proposing that being creative with an imaging program on a computer is like manipulating the immaterial and the ethereal. Provided, that is, we remember Master Chuang`s advice, and do not allow things to use *us* as things. The very lack of contact with the medium – for the medium in this case is electricity and light – allows us to distance our physical selves, placing us in the fortunate position of not requiring manual dexterity and fine

CITY
by Chris Turner
(Clapham Park
School) standard
page 320 x 256
pixels

we are doing is not something precious, in the sense of a scarce product or unrepeatable performance, but fluid, protean, organic, infinitely perfectible. And the resulting print seems less of a physical presence, for it is not the record of a constructed struggle with pigment, but rather a reminder of a journey, a dream sectioned and stained for scrutiny, the precipitate of this alchemy of light.

An introverted attitude, therefore, which withdraws its emphasis from the external world (the world of consciousness) and localises it in the subjective factor (the background of consciousness) necessarily calls forth the characteristic manifestations of the unconscious, namely, archaic thought-forms imbued with 'ancestral' or 'historic' feeling, and, beyond them, the sense of infiniteness, timelessness, oneness.[7]

motor control but needing rather clarity of vision and patient application, thus placing us, in a very real sense, in a meditative position. We begin to see the inadequacy of 'painting' as a term for this new medium, and the aptness of imaging or image manipulation, or even image processing[6] (for it repays comparison with word processing). You the reader do not know whether this sentence came first or last in the order of creating this paragraph, nor do you know whether I use the keyboard as a skilled typist or with my big toe. I do not need to have a clear idea to begin with nor need I have an easy way with words. All that I require is the ability to recognise that something is unclear or could be better expressed. The sentences and paragraphs grow slowly and the ideas crystallise out. If I choose to delete this word or this sentence or this paragraph it can disappear without trace. If I clear the screen accidentally, I can recall this document in the form in which I last saved it. Any part can be picked up and pushed around. Anything done can be undone.

So too the image. It exists as a coded signal, saved on a disk, to be resurrected when I choose. It can exist on several disks, or the same image can be loaded from a single disk onto several machines. And this too encourages the realisation that what

With or without acceptance of the objective psyche and the archetypes, we can use the passage from Jung as a paradigm for the situation of someone seated before a blank black monitor screen about to use an imaging program. It is like staring into our deep dark well, a state of sensory deprivation, introverted precisely because there are no apparent co-ordinates. Perfect for the unconscious to manifest. And, as in a dream, any manifestation, any fragment can move, grow to fill the screen, our field of vision, or shrink to invisibility. Any motif can be recalled to contaminate any other, like the varied ripples on the surface of a pool interlinking, just as new ideas impinge upon all our thinking. This, I believe, is one of the reasons why a good imaging program has the power to unlock the imagination and liberate creativity. Granted that it takes time and practice to gain the familiarity needed before it is possible to feel relaxed and confident and comfortable, but then the hand is almost lost as the mind's eye finds, building images of numinous freshness. Cunning contrivances can result in cunning performances and in the process provide a restorative for the quiet of the soul.

Artisan Ch`ui could draw as true as a compass or a T-square because his fingers changed along with things and he didn't let his mind get in the way. Therefore his Spirit Tower remained unified and unobstructed.

You forget your feet when the shoes are comfortable. You forget your waist when the belt is comfortable. There is no change to what is inside, no following what is outside, when the adjustment to events is comfortable. You begin with what is comfortable and never experience what is uncomfortable when you know the comfort of forgetting what is comfortable.[8]

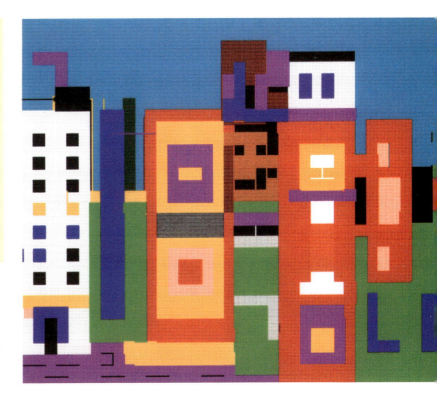

Having become familiar with the basics of an imaging program we must now introduce it to the students. A possible starting point is the creation of a cityscape using filled rectangles for towers and windows, building with blocks of colour. This may seem a somewhat soulless and mechanical exercise but to students new to the medium it should be challenging enough, and it can give a surprisingly clear indication of many things, because it requires discipline to select only colours, and to create only rectangles of various sizes proportionate to each other. Clouds may be added to the sky later, using a large brush functioning as an airbrush.

It is important to make this first experience a positive one. To use the program in this limited way is to succeed. The aim is not to create masterpieces of startling originality – that can come later. And if all the works have a sameness about them at this stage, so much the better, for this allows the teacher to feel free to intervene to demonstrate the program on an individual basis, ensuring, for example, that the students are clear about saving and re-saving their work at regular intervals. This is the safety net, their security, and it should dispel any feelings of preciousness toward the screen image, which is vital if the students are to become sufficiently experimental. This sameness also helps establish group ownership of the idea, which becomes increasingly important, for it allows the students to learn from one another's discoveries. A new idea, or a new way of using a particular function, instantly becomes collective property and collective responsibility for future development.

Other things may become apparent in retrospect. For example it can be seen that Isaac's work remains very flat spatially whereas Chris has a remarkable feel for the spatial existence of patches of colour and this is already evident in his city picture with its clear demarcation between foreground and distant shapes.

Chris went on to produce **LIMO**, beautiful for its simplicity of composition and controlled use of a limited palette and bold shapes that echo each other, capturing something of the essence of night-empty streets. Millions of colours are not necessarily a prerequisite for usefulness in an imaging program. His Robocop video cover can be seen to be another exploration of the same theme. Both pictures demonstrate Chris's extraordinary spatial ability. He paints abstract patches of colour and thinks quite clearly about their relative positions in space and he peoples the space accordingly.

After the desolation of the city it is useful to introduce a landscape theme, a growing tree perhaps, where students are asked to create forms more freely, sinuously, as though alive and growing. They can also add animals or people.

CITY
by Mary Cameron
(Clapham Park School)
standard page 320 x
256 pixels

LIMO
by Chris Turner
(Clapham Park School)
standard page 320 x
256 pixels

Below: **ROBOCOP**
video cover by Chris
Turner (Clapham Park
School) standard page
320 x 256 pixels

Bottom:

DRAGON by mary
Cameron (Clapham
Park School) standard
page 320 x 256 pixels)

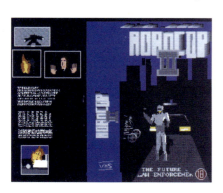

The human form may be more problematic for some of the students. Previous failure to achieve satisfactory results may have led them to shy away from attempting its representation. I am reminded of a friend's anecdote of his experience of teaching young children. 'If I asked them to draw a man, they couldn't. And if I asked them to draw an elephant, they couldn't. But if I asked them to draw a man on an elephant they would do it.'[9] It's a nice observation, and it contains a grain of truth. We present the students with the starting point for a fresh journey, as though we give them a map. But there is no map, there is only the starting point based on trust, for it is a journey into the unknown.

Duwney changed **JUNGLE HEAT** and saved it as **STING**, which I thought strange but Duwney obviously had his own idea. We then had a half-term holiday. After the holiday he created the rabbit and the figure, and the following week the bees. Only then did it become clear that the title of the picture referred to the fact that the woman bending down to look at the rabbit was about to have a bee sting her in the bottom.

A work of art can excite us intellectually and ignite our instincts but for a painting or sculpture to do so it must be experienced as a physical presence in its own particular scale and for its own particular tactile qualities. At Thurlow Park School we try to visit museums regularly and to have the students regard them as places of fun and refuge. A favoured approach is to seek out works rich in the symbolism of classical mythology or Christian iconography, although Hogarth and many Pre-Raphaelite paintings present an equally fertile hunting ground. One of our visits to the oriental

JUNGLE HEAT
and **STING**
by Duwney Clarke
(Clapham Park School)
standard page 320 x
256 pixels

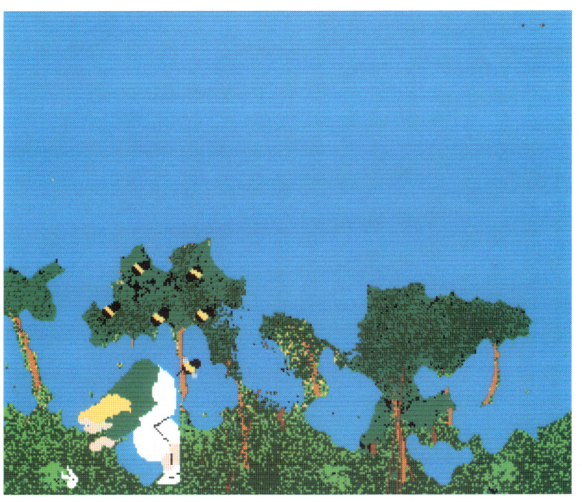

DAVID NICHOLLS

BOY

by Isaac Williams
(Clapham Park School)
standard page 320 x
256 pixels

Below: **TREE**

by Isaac Williams
(Clapham Park School)
standard page 320 x
256 pixels

galleries at the British Museum to study Hindu sacred sculpture resulted in the production of half animal half human forms. This had the added advantage of making distortion and ambiguity acceptable. thus avoiding anxiety, a variation of the man on an elephant trick. You may object that this is a very superficial approach to Hinduism,[10] and yes, in a way, it is. But if it gives a student a strategy for achieving something then it is a positive approach and, presumably, a memorable one. In the case of Derek, who had quite a struggle to control what he was doing, the images resulting from his struggle have an eerie presence and charm.

It is of course impossible for many schools to visit museums so one must resort to reproductions. I have never cared for copying as such nor for those exercises 'in the style of', although they no doubt help students to look more carefully. But we regularly use line illustrations as source material and I think the **SPHINXES** by Ricky and Steve speak for themselves. There is no sameness there, even though the starting point was identical.[11]

MANFISH

by Derek Ayi (Clapham
Park School) standard
page 320 x 256 pixels

VISHNU

by Derek Ayi (Clapham
Park School) standard
page 320 x 256 pixels

SPHINX

by Roberto Caballero
(Thurlow Park School)
extend page 608 x 500
pixels

SPHINX

by Stephen Sadler
(Thurlow Park School)
extended page 640 x
512 pixels

CRAB

by Kalwant Gill
(Clapham Park School)
standard page 320 x
256 pixels

SEASIDE

by Hitan Patel
(Thurlow Park School)
standard page 320 x
256 pixels

Another possibility is the use of astrological symbolism. Kalwant's **CRAB** is based on his own birth-sign Cancer. The element is water, under the influence of the moon. Kalwant became fascinated by patterns of water-rippled light and worked this leitmotif into his pictures whenever he could. My favourite remains this crab nibbling the reflected moon.

Once confidence is established, it is surprising how individual each artist's work becomes, possibly much more so than with conventional media. A comparison of Hitan's **SEASIDE** with Nguyet's **BEACH** illustrates this quite clearly.

Nguyet became so involved with the texture of the sand that it flies everywhere and the figures at the top left of the picture seem to swirl with it in a rapture of sunbathing. Hitan, on the other hand, had to learn to accept distortion as an antidote to *the straight line perfectibility trap*. This malady is usually caused by the too-early overuse of the zoom function, working with 'magnified' pixels as though bricklaying instead of drawing freely. It has

its uses for final details but it is as well to be on guard for its pitfalls.

Robert's **THE EXPELLED** (Adam & Eve) is a good example of how acceptance of distortion and lack of finish can actually add to the expressiveness

It might be objected that I read too much into these images, that this was never the artist's intention, that what I see as panache is simply lack of finish, accidental, chance. But it is a vital dimension of art, and art education, that we learn to interpret images – hence our study of symbolism. And it is vital for them as artists to experiment and to accept serendipity. Artists choose what they will leave as the final image and in this way 'chance' becomes purposive. Alternative interpretation becomes an added impetus to invention and our intention also evolves. As creative human beings we constantly interrogate ourselves in relation to the world, our world. And art, like life, is not a rehearsal; this is the real thing. We are not learning to be creative, we are being creative. And learning is creative, because for each of us it is an individual synthesis.

BEACH

by Nguyet Truong (Thurlow Park School) standard page 320 x 256 pixels

of the picture. This is a very sudden and shocking expulsion. The drama could so easily have been lost by over refinement (not that refinement was ever Robert's style!).[12] The stance of the figures may also owe something to Isaac's **BOY**.

Diego's picture began as an aimless swirl of colour but immediately suggested a mother and child, the mother arching over the baby, in a way reminiscent of **NUT**, Ancient Egyptian goddess of the sky (especially as painted on the ceiling of the tomb of

THE EXPELLED

by Robert Osborne (Thurlow Park School) extended page 640 x 512 pixels

NUT

by Diego Soto
(Thurlow Park School)
standard page 320 x
256 pixels

GREY RIVER

by Raymond Kilden (Thurlow Park School) standard page
320 x 256 pixels

Rameses VI). Diego[13] chose not to go on with this
picture, preferring a more intellectual approach, but
then tended to get bogged down in zoom,
perfecting every minor detail.

Raymond would often begin a session by doodling
rapidly with the mouse, clearing the screen, then
doodling again, as though to assert his control.
Sometimes these doodles would suggest images,
which could then be clarified, teased out gradually.
GREY RIVER began as one such doodle which
Raymond then extended as **GREY REFLECTED**.

GREY REFLECTED

by Raymond Kilden (Thurlow Park School) standard page
320 x 256 pixels

LION AMOK, shown with its originating doodle, is a splendidly dynamic composition. This image grew very slowly over many weeks as Raymond abandoned it for a while to work on other images or to draw from observation on paper.

But work from observation need not necessarily be on paper. We should not forget that it is just as valid a discipline to draw from observation using a mouse or trackball in a painting program. This drawing can then feed the work from imagination.

LION AMOK
by Raymond Kilden (Thurlow Park School)
standard page 320 x 256 pixels

The students did an observation of a human skull and then some work from a complete human skeleton. This in turn was followed by a visit to the Museum of Mankind for the exhibition: *The Skeleton at the Feast*, a celebration of the Mexican Day of the Dead. I asked them to turn their observational studies to comic effect and, as usual, they rose to the challenge. Kalwant's **FRED&GINGER** is in my view a comic masterpiece, perfectly in tune with the spirit of the exhibition. The low-resolution coarseness of the images adds a handmade handbuilt look and feel that the students respond to in a very positive way, giving the final prints the texture of tapestry. This tactile quality is most evident in **SKELETON**, a picture that gains significantly by being printed as an enlargement. Many people have initially reacted to the print by reaching out to run their fingers over the pixel stitching. Which brings us to some important technical considerations.

PARTRIDGE
by Nguyet Truong (Thurlow Park School) page size 320 x 400 pixels

I have tried to avoid technical vocabulary as far as possible. The aim of this study is to present the case for using imaging programs, by showing examples of the way we have structured the work at Thurlow Park School, evolving one method from another. I have not attempted a guided tour of the various functions one can expect from an imaging program. Such works already exist, although I believe the best place for that sort of tour is in the manual specific to the program you intend to use. The manual is designed to be worked through systematically using the program and loading the examples, following the exercises. Only in this way will it be memorable. However, if you are seriously intending introducing electronic imaging into your art practice but have not yet decided which program to use, one thing you should look for is the ability to change the size and

FREDnGINGER
by Kalwant Gill (Clapham Park School) extended page 368 x 256 pixels

17

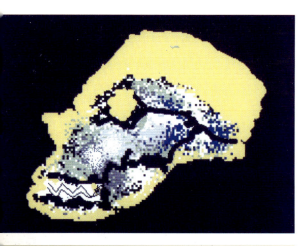

SKULL

by Robert Osborne
(Thurlow Park
School) standard
page 320 x 256 pixels

SKULL

by Raymond Kilden
(Thurlow Park
School) standard
page 320 x 256 pixels

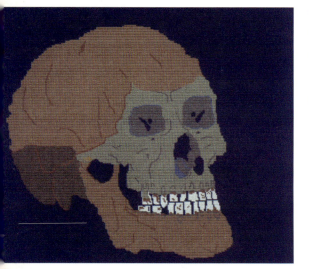

SKULL

by Ricardo Caballero
(Thurlow Park
School) standard
page 320 x 256 pixels

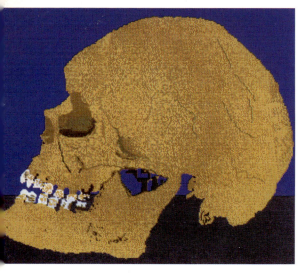

SKULL

by Stephen Sadler
(Thurlow Park
School) standard
page 320 x 256 pixels

shape of your working page, and you should be able to do this simply by locating through the menu the appropriate dialogue box and then keying in the desired page size in pixel dimension. With **SKELETON** Robert worked until the skull and rib cage filled the screen, then added an additional 256 pixels, effectively doubling the height of his working page, worked some more, added some more, and so on. In this way the page grows to accommodate the developing composition, the artist scrolling through the extended page vertically and/or horizontally just as one would when processing a lengthy document.

Having established that your program has this facility you should then ensure that it, or an additional compatible program, allows you to print it out in a variety of sizes. And be sure to have a good quality printer.

A simple way of introducing the extended page is to have the students design the top half of a playing card, filling the screen. Once this is achieved, the page height can be doubled and the design copied as a brush, turned through 180 degrees, placed on the lower half of the page, and then the midline reworked to ensure continuity.

Your program may also allow you to produce simple page-turning animation. One lunchtime Robert produced a figure by drawing in bilateral symmetry. He returned to the figure later and animated it over six frames by varying the angles of the arms and adding the red and blue balls. When played as an animation with the colour cycling, the showbiz suit sparkles. This is animation as an exercise for its own sake. The six frames (here arranged and printed as a static picture, with the originating figure in the centre) run as a loop, the movement constantly repeating. When doing animation for the first time it is useful to consider that certain movements can work very well as a loop, such as Robert's **BOUNCE**, or a person juggling, or a swing, a seesaw, or skipping.

When the students had successfully peopled their pictures I became concerned that too many of the figures were flat and unimaginative, drawn either in profile or full face. I thought animation might help remedy this and so asked the students to create a turning head. This requires the head to be drawn in five positions – front face, three-quarter front, profile, three-quarter back, back. The profile and three-quarter views can be flipped horizontally to complete the turn. The views are then placed on the same point on eight pages. When played as an animation the head appears to turn.

The students were asked to use this new development in a figure composition so that figures were created as seen from various positions: people at a party, standing, talking, or people round a table, eating or planning. Ricky's **CONSPIRATORS** was one of the best images to come out of this exercise, but Steve's **SELF PORTRAIT** probably owed something to this exercise. Having established the main elements of the picture through observation, he made alterations and additions for purely aesthetic reasons.

All data used by a computer must be in digital form. Photographs or video images can be scanned or grabbed in various ways but, to be used on the computer, they must be transformed, digitised. When we first set up our imaging system we included a video digitiser. This piece of hardware and its accompanying software form the connection between a video camera and a computer and enable one to grab video images, live or from video cassette. An image once grabbed, if considered satisfactory, can be digitised. Once digitised and saved it can be loaded into an imaging program and manipulated. This is clearly a powerful device but using digitised imagery in a creative way proved more problematic, and the digitiser, after several dead end attempts, lay unused for a while. For what is one to do with a digitised image? A digitiser can transform an image in a very painterly way but the image is perfect in itself. And of course it is now possible to take pictures with a video stills camera.

SKELETON

by Robert Osborne (Thurlow Park School) extended page 320 x 740 pixels

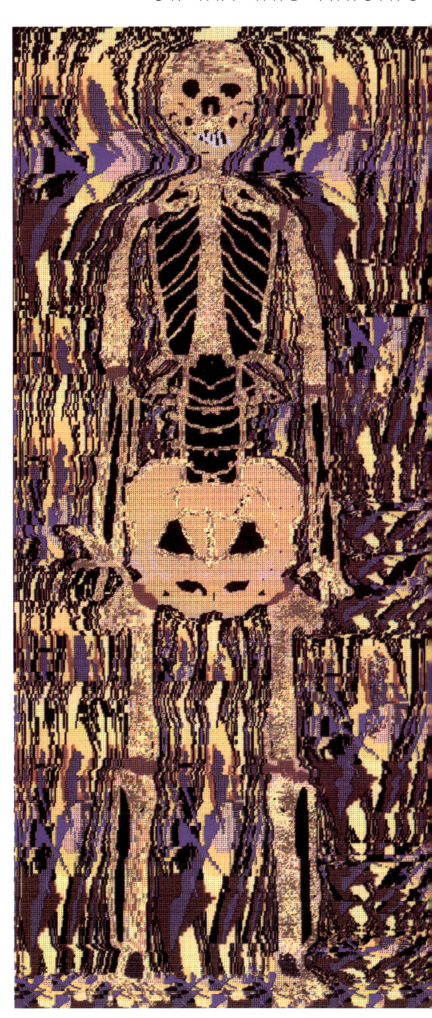

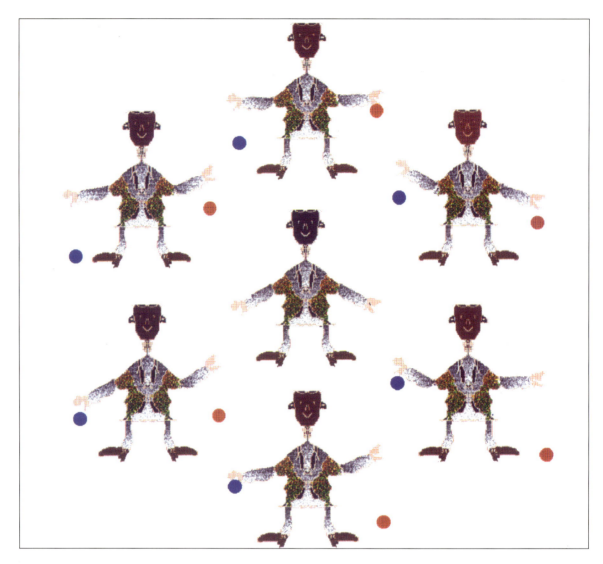

BOUNCE

by Robert Osborne
(Thurlow Park School)
extended page 608 x
600 pixels

Some time ago we based a project on the local cemetery, using digitised imagery. The cemetery is noted for its Victorian funerary monuments. Chris treated his chosen image quite roughly and this is a good attitude to have. The bats take over the picture and the digitised image is relegated to the background. In the context of Chris's work it is a one off. It did not stem from anything else and, while Chris was with us, it did not lead to anything more. And I failed to see at the time that this is exactly how to treat digitised imagery.

TURNING HEAD

by Stephen Sadler
(Thurlow Park School)
originally created as an
eight frame animation

TUBE by Duwney Clarke (Clapham Park School) standard page 320 x 256 pixels.

Duwney animated his TUBE character, which became useful later when he used individual figures to people other pictures.

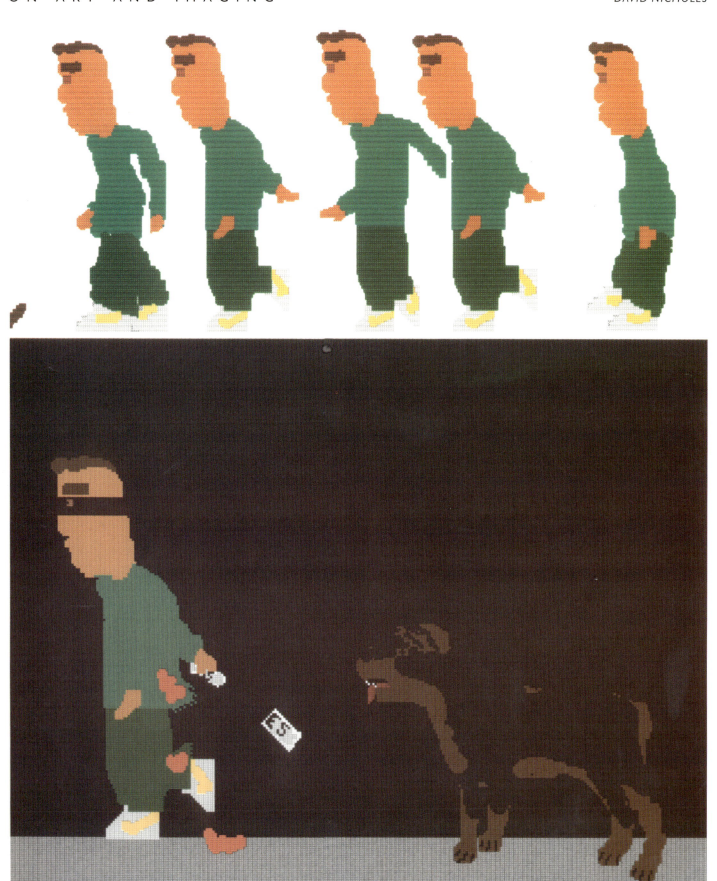

DOG by Duwney Clark (Clapham Park School) standard page 320 x 256 pixels.

The most remarkable thing about this picture, however, is that it began with the dog, drawn as disconnected brown patches on a blank black screen.

SELF PORTRAIT by Stephen Sadler (Thurlow Park School) extended page 384 x 530 pixels

CONSPIRATORS

by Ricardo Caballero
(Thurlow Park School)
standard page 320 x
256 pixels

DALTON

by Chris Turner
(Clapham Park School)
standard page 320 x
256 pixels

Enlarged detail from
STONE ANGEL
by Oliver Conmee

STONE ANGEL on the other hand is perhaps not such a successful picture. Oliver did not have a strong enough idea and I had not given him one, so he filled a bit and drew a bit, even created the figure, which I printed out as an isolated enlargement and asked him about. He told me it was a devil. We both agreed that it wasn't very devilish and that he might try to do something about that as a separate picture. So then he just let the **DEVIL** happen, a very strange image, and so marvellously devilish you can almost smell the brimstone. But then what is that bear doing in the devil picture? So he went away again. And so on.

Ideally it becomes a dialogue with the possibilities of the medium, just as teaching is a dialogue with the possibilities of the students. It is always traversing the same ground, always approaching the same problems but from different angles, through different subjects.

The same or almost the same points were always being approached afresh from different directions, and new sketches made. Very many of these were badly drawn or uncharacteristic, marked by all the defects of a weak draughtsman. And when they were rejected a number of tolerable ones were left, which now had to be arranged and sometimes cut down, so that if you looked at them you could get a picture of a landscape. Thus this book is really only an album.[14]

Wittgenstein offers this analogy by way of apology, but isn't this how we build our own philosophy — piecemeal, revising in the light of experience, refining our approximation? Except that with aesthetics, and ethics, we assume greater choice,

STONE ANGEL
by Oliver Conmee
(Thurlow Park School)
extended page 624 x 620 pixels

DEVIL (& BEAR)
by Oliver Conmee (Thurlow Park School) extended page 320 x 280 pixels

less a natural landscape and more a cultivated garden, even though our aim may in some cases be a 'natural' feel. The garden will never be absolutely right. It will always require tending and weeding to keep it alive. Always need walking in to give it meaning.

We can probably remember our own creations when we were at school, how sometimes the paint or the colour or the composition seemed beyond our control. This was because it really was beyond our control, because painting a picture is a complex intuitive process (I use the word intuitive in the Kantian sense, that is, making an informed judgement based on our sensory awareness). Just how complex it can be is continually made fresh to us as teachers. For example, a student is trying to paint a portrait from observation but is obviously dissatisfied: the proportions are all wrong and the skin colours are distinctly Fauve, which is not the object of the exercise that day. We sit down and quickly mix the flesh tones, as they appear in the light of the art room, and do a quick rough sketch on which to perpetrate various anomalies by way of demonstration. But the student can see that the sketch bears a striking resemblance to the model and sees that the colour looks 'real' and asks: How do you do that? So we postpone the demonstration we were going to do, and backtrack and start again. this time talking it through. But we are unable to talk it through, or can do so only partially, because the colour mixing takes on massive proportions and the measuring of the model even more. The problem is there, occupying our concentration fully but largely without recourse to language. The sudden dawnings of realisation born of patient application, and the words that resonated our own understanding those many years ago, have long since sunk without trace. There is only the understanding, and the dexterity, and the sensitivity, built in over years of drawing and measuring and looking. Our attention shifting and sifting, now analysing the reflected light, now the underlying structure, now the proportion of part to whole, and so on. It is that kind of holistic thinking we are aiming for with our students. It is that which we attempt to reconstruct in our

Opposite:

PRIZEWINNING POSTER

by Stephen Sadler (Stonehenge) Georgina Fitch (Big Ben) Tony Jukes (Castle) Nguyet Truong (Pavilion) and Owen Attard (Viaduct and Tudor House). (Thurlow Park School) extended page 672 x 1000 pixels

teaching. And it is that attempted reconstruction in language that can make teaching such a rich learning experience for us. As creative human beings we constantly interrogate ourselves in relation to the world, our world.

"Not, however, as if to this end we had to hunt out new facts; it is, rather, of the essence of our investigation that we do not seek to learn anything new by it. We want to understand something that is already in plain view. For this is what we seem in some sense not to understand... Something that we know when no one asks us, but no longer know when we are supposed to give an account of it, is something that we need to remind ourselves of: (And it is obviously something of which for some reason it is difficult to remind oneself)'.[15]

In the early days of television – well, the mid-1950s, – there was a public service program, a short moralising animation, urging people to save. Money in the bank was compared to planting an apple seed in the ground. The impatient character kept sneaking out at night to dig up his seed and make sure it was still there, so of course it never grew. The smart character slept at night and eventually, very quickly in the animation, enjoyed the fruits of his mature investment. I have never learned to save although I accept that learning is saving, with interest. We drop our coin into the well expecting and accepting increase.

When teaching the younger children I often begin a session by leading a group through a procedure in stages. The knack is to find some device that does not require lengthy explanation. In isolation this may seem too controlled by me, too much of an imposition from without, but it has proved a useful way of making steps to other things. And by ensuring an end product we establish trust and self-belief. The **CITY** pictures with which we began can be seen to be based on the same principle. So far as I am concerned the momentum is the important thing. Giving a push to let go. And sometimes the intended outcome of the process I am leading them through is a mystery to them until the end. By keeping them in the dark I contrive to prevent their preconceptions or their worries

SAVE YESTERDAYS

CREATION TODAY

FOR TOMORROW

Media Save Art 1993

getting in the way. Our aim is an acceptance of the symbolic possibilities of abstract marks. Their final position is the important thing. The patch of blue we are painting may stand for sea or for sky, depending on which way up we finally have the paper. The holes we are pressing into a slab of clay may stand for falling leaves or falling snow. The truly creative is a surprise, especially to the creator. Out of darkness grows enlightenment, but the darkness must be carefully primed.

It is essential to be relaxed and accepting of change, to have fun, because tension can block creativity. If a child engaged in symbolic play were asked constantly to explain every step of the way then play would cease. The requirement that we analyse what we are doing gets in the way of our ability to synthesise. As with the uncertainty principle, by analysing position we lose momentum. Continually digging up the seed aborts germination. With the computer we are not suddenly required to think in a different way, a machinelike way based on jargon. The creative process is not suddenly clear to our reason, to the fore in our consciousness, as though there were some logic by which to justify it. This causes only confusion and confusion failure, because of striving for an impossible clarity. There is no synthetic syllogism because there are no surprises in logic. The computer can act as a prop to our memory and to our creativity but it does not do the thinking for us. We need therefore to revise just what it is we do and how it is we are able to be creative. When using the machine we should always look to the spirit in which we use it.

It was Piaget who coined the oft-quoted line that play is child's work. ... the other half of this pithy aphorism [is] the idea that work (at least serious intellectual work) might be adult's play. We thought of children as 'little scientists' but did not think much about the complementary idea of viewing scientists as 'big children'.[16]

And just like 'little scientists', 'big children' can also get stuck[17] and become uncreative, measuring position and losing momentum. Richard Feynman has written about his own experience of breaking through this block.

...So I decided I'm going to do things only for the fun of it.

That afternoon while I was eating lunch some kid threw up a plate in the cafeteria. There was a blue medallion on the plate, the Cornell sign, and as he threw up the plate and it came down, the blue thing went around and it seemed to me that the blue thing went around faster than the wobble, and I wondered what the relation was between the two. I was just playing, no importance at all, but I played around with the equations of motion of rotating things, and I found out that if the wobble is small the blue thing goes around twice as fast as the wobble goes round. Then I tried to figure out if I could see why that was directly from Newton's laws instead of through the complicated equations, and I worked that out for the fun of it.

... I started to play with this rotation, and the rotation led me to a similar problem of the rotation of the spin of an electron according to Dirac's equation, and that just led me back into quantum electrodynamics, which was the problem I had been working on. I kept continuing now to play with it in the relaxed fashion I had originally done, and it was just like taking the cork out of a bottle — everything just poured out, and in very short order I worked the things out for which I later won the Nobel Prize.[18]

The ability to be playful and to have fun is our antidote to the creative block. An imaging program is in a sense the ultimate playground for the artist, for just as for a child a cardboard box can be now a car, now a horse, now a submarine, so the program enables limitless transformations thus encouraging movement and serendipity as opposed to the striving to attain an impossible grammar.

So long as there is momentum there is life and the possibility of growth. With a painting program the tools are there, the powers are there, to be discovered in playful exploration. The student can try various effects, swapping and changing tools, being experimental for its own sake, continually making the image afresh, without risk. Developing a feel for the program that is not dependent on language. But to achieve this we need to give up the notion of being in control, which for some, for historical reasons,[19] is not so easy with computers.

The object of a technology lesson in a mainstream girls' school was to determine how many pennyweights could be carried by a given cube of expanded polystyrene floated in a tank of water. Most of the girls dutifully started by placing weights, one after another, on top of their cube until it became top-heavy and rolled, toppling the weights into the water. Then they made a hollow in one face of the cube and tried again, and so on,. One girl opted out, refused to join in, was bored. Eventually the other students had all made a primitive boat which could carry a number of weights without toppling. The bored girl then took up her piece of polystyrene and proceeded to force weights edgeways into every face of the cube until it could accommodate no more. She then lobbed it into the water and of course it floated. The teacher however, exclaimed: 'Oh no, that's not what we are doing!'

If we approach teaching thus it is as though we intend students to learn in a linear fashion only what the curriculum prescribes for that particular slot or that we teach only that which can be easily recorded for assessment purposes. We do not float through life simply filling our empty vessel with pennyweights of dead information. The aim of all worthwhile education is that it nurtures independent inventiveness so that we come to see that everything relates to who we are, where we are. The personal response, the personal discovery, is of prime importance. With computers especially, the students will usually outstrip us in expertise and confidence of handling. We need to be prepared for this, to accept it, to enjoy learning from them in an atmosphere of student autonomy and mutual respect. Teaching is not something to be mechanically delivered; learning is not something to be passively received. We know this, so let us not be thrown when we come into contact with the machine. We must not allow ourselves to be used by things.

My theory is that the best way to teach is to have no philosophy, to be chaotic and confuse it in the sense that you use every possible way of doing it. That's the only way I can see, to catch this guy and that guy on different hooks as you go along.[20]

When I first started teaching, in a mainstream school for girls, Kay, one of the students in the examination group, brought a folder of work that looked to me absolutely static. Much of it consisted of overlapping circles and squares and triangles drawn in a mechanical way with a hard pencil and then feebly coloured in with watery paint. The turning point for Kay came when she rediscovered her playfulness and trust in herself. As a loosening up exercise, when we were painting I urged the group to lay the paint on really thick, to enjoy it, if they could, for its own sake, to relinquish their control of the medium and allow themselves to be messy. Kay eventually started rubbing her hands in the paint, the sort of thing we do in the nursery, and then checked herself and asked me if she was allowed to do it like that. I assured her that if she was enjoying it, that was fine. So she carried on, or rather she plunged in. From then on she loved using rich colour and thick paint (with a brush) and became a very good painter. Her drawing also became very strong – she was a delight to teach. I would sometimes set up a large still-life in the centre of the art room for the groups to paint. One day the examination group came in, got their materials, sat down and started to paint. All except Kay. She did not feel like doing it that day. I asked her what she wanted to do and she replied that she would like to read. So that is what she did. While the other twenty-three girls settled down to grapple with the still-life, Kay sat on the fitted worktop at the back of the room and read her book – for about ten minutes. Then she jumped down, said, 'I've got an idea', and proceeded to paint the subject in the confident manner to which we had both become accustomed. I realise that with another group my approach could have been disastrous, but I tell the story to demonstrate the importance of being able to turn away from a problem so as to look back and see it afresh, and

The grid devised by
Geoff Cox

	of Derek	of Georgina	of Hitan	of Mary	of Nguyet	of Stephen	of Tony
by Derek	thoughtful	weird, the things you say, the things you do	shy, but not with friends	is a storywriter	is a fidget	forgetful	talkative
by Georgina	mad	unpredictable	likes going out with friends	likes a laugh	likes beating up boys	likes saying peace	likes to moan
by Hitan	calm	mad	likes video games	quite tough outside and inside doesn't get hurt by jokes	always falling over	likes throwing pencils and rubbers about -	forgetful
by Mary	vain	helpful	very polite never a rude word	likes reading	likes boys	friendly	acts tough, thinks he's tough
by Nguyet	eats a lot	looks like a boy	is very quiet	likes a good natter	likes art	always talkative	never shuts up
by Stephen	impatient	not everyday unusual	has a lot of football knowledge	likes music	wears loud clothes	likes football	is lovely and chubby
by Tony	big	Chelsea fan	neat and tidy, fashionable	eccentric not everyday hairstyle	serious, down to earth	sticks tongue out when concentrating	likes eating

Below:

Detail of the final collage: Derek's realisation of 'vain' (of Derek by Mary)

the need for teachers to have strategies to accommodate that process. The still-life set-up in question was somewhat unusual, if I remember correctly, with hanging sheets of unrolled kitchen foil and steel containers and mirrors. Kay had arrived fresh but unprepared. It looked to her like a completely new problem. She just needed that bit of time to plant the seed, to let it sink in, to let the penny drop. We have to lose sight of it, to let go of it, so that we can bring it back fresh with interest. Sometimes the most positive course is inactivity, detachment, doing nothing, waiting.

Now, patience; and remember patience is the great thing, and above all things else we must try to avoid anything like being or becoming out of patience.[21]

It took time to build up our own expertise, and it may take our students time.

One criterion for measuring the success of a piece of work or a particular project could be consideration of whether it helps evolve and feed general practice – pretty much the principle I have adopted here. In which case it is a good idea to print examples of such work and keep them in a display folder for reference. The students are thus made aware of the tradition which they are establishing and upon which they are building, which in turn may help them in their approach to art history and aesthetics.

In 1993 we were offered funding for a project in association with Photofusion.[22] This gave us the opportunity to explore the possibility of enriching electronic imaging through photography and related techniques. It was hoped that parallel development would lead to cross-fertilisation. The art sessions thus became mixed sessions – sometimes the photographic element would dominate and sometimes the electronic imaging. Geoff Cox, the resident artist for the first year of the project, began in the most straightforward way, arranging for us to take simple monochrome portrait shots with a 35mm SLR camera mounted on a tripod. All the students and Geoff and I had our portraits taken in the same sequence, viz., full face, profile, then free choice of pose. The film was taken away for processing. The printed photographs provided the basis for the next camera session. After looking at the monochrome portraits and discussing their sameness of framing and pose and exposure, he gave the students compact cameras with colour film and suggested that they try to take bad photographs of each other, or perhaps one should say idiosyncratic photographs, like the world's worst amateur, with crazy angles and missing heads and lack of focus. Instead of touring a gallery and stopping to unpack various images, the students were approaching considerations of composition and intention in a very direct way. They were making decisions about framing their shots in a way that they would not have were they simply taking snapshots of each other. Usually the only consideration when taking a snapshot is that the subject can be seen. The person or group becomes the target and the viewfinder becomes the sight for aiming. So long as there is a head dead centre the

Above: Collage of 42 inches square

Left: Detail (six inch square) Georgina by Steve 'not everyday, unusual'

shot is on target. The surroundings become an irrelevance. The only object is to make a killing, to secure a trophy on film.

Next, he asked the seven students each to make one comment about themselves and their own character, and one comment about the character of each of the other members of the group. These comments were transposed onto a grid and this grid translated into a large photographic collage.

Nguyet becoming
Mary

Multiple exposures
created with Geoff
Cox and a large format
camera

Below: Steve juggling

After experimenting with photographic images projected from slides onto the students and then photographing the projected-upon students, work began on the computers. Each student worked with his or her own image, digitised through the video camera, trying to juxtapose it in some revelatory way with images of stone-carved gargoyles, already digitised in the same way.

This was followed by more experimental techniques, including photographing the students in costume. Steadily the work became more self-exploratory and individualised. The work of two of our artists makes this clear, so is now described in greater detail.

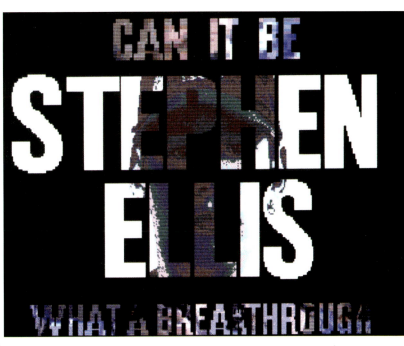

Above: Stone carved head. This, and many other carved images, was digitised for us by Jason Lyne.

Top right: **BREAKTHROUGH** by Stephen Sadler (formerly Stephen Ellis) standard page 320 x 256 pixels Steve uses the same digitised image of himself combined with a brilliant use of lettering.

Right: **LION**
by Stephen Sadler (Thurlow School)
extended page 320 x 515 pixels
LION is a memorable if somewhat disturbing image reminiscent of the photomontage of John Heartfield.

SAVE OUR GARGOYLES

by Tony Jukes

page 400 x 256 pixels

Tony

Tony was familiar with Deluxe Paint long before he began the GCSE course but it was always a considerable struggle for him. And he continued to struggle, every image being agonised over, almost tortured into existence. But he had a strong desire to do it, and his great sense of humour and streetwise chat were clear indications of his mercurial wit, so the prospect was good. His first big success came with **SAVE OUR GARGOYLES**, which he designed for the poster competition Your Past Our Future organised by the Accademia Italiana. It was a fun idea, a solo effort, (as opposed to the group poster on which he had collaborated

the previous year) and it won £500 for the art department. This was a turning point for Tony. He suddenly realised the fun in being creative. He has never looked back, and his work has gone from strength to strength. After struggling for so long, at last he had self-belief as an artist. He took readily to using digitised imagery as his raw material. It was, after all, his short cut to success, and he continued to treat it in a cavalier fashion, which is, I now realise, the only way to break away from its ready-made perfection.

His next venture was a series of pictures each beginning with his own digitised image, which he manipulated in various ways to make a collection of designs for music CDs. All the pictures are designed in a circle with the song titles integral to the design.

Combining text and image was an area that continued to occupy my thinking and clearly there had been some notable successes with posters and video covers. So while Tony continued to work on individual ideas I had him dictate to me various statements about himself that I hoped would lead to further self-exploration. Once the text was in place it suddenly seemed to pull everything together. The words stimulated the programme

FUNNY MONEY

by Tony Jukes

(Thurlow Park School)

extended page 448 x 256 pixels

Tony's text

I like a laugh.

I like food.

I'm a good artist.

I play the clown occasionally in school.

I like football.

I love it when Chelsea score and I would love it if England won something.

I love football when they have a fight.

I like an argument.

I went to my aunt's in Nottingham. I was only there one day. It was my uncle's birthday and we had a barbecue with all his friends from work. It started raining so we all went to the pub. I had a swear pot and every time they swore they had to put money in it. I went in with about twenty quid.

A Chelsea supporter went round with the pot for me and I finished up with seventy-three quid.

I love money.

I'm a con artist.

I've got a cousin who says that in one ear she can hear god talking to her, and in the other ear she can hear the devil talking to her. Which one does she listen to? The devil of course. She's only seven.

Oi! What do you want?

I've only been kicked out of one cinema.

and accelerated production of the final images, and the creative process became very much a two-way thing between words and pictures. It was another significant leap for Tony, and he was visibly and contagiously excited as the connections were made and the ideas poured out.

The ideal perhaps would be to manipulate the images in multimedia authoring software, to create a composite interactive self-portrait incorporating animation and sound, where the images dissolve from one to another in time to Tony's recorded voice saying his text. We are now equipped with a multimedia PC486, and we hope eventually to find the time to do that... although I have some reservations.

There is a definition of a lecture as the process whereby the notes of the lecturer become the notes of the student without passing through the mind of either. Downloading images and texts from

FRY UP

by Tony Jukes (Thurlow Park School) extended page 352 x 444 pixels competition poster

you are what you eat......

ANGEL
by Tony Jukes
(Thurlow Park
School) standard
page 320 x 256
pixels

CLOWN
by Tony Jukes
(Thurlow Park
School) standard
page 320 x 256
pixels

CDROM or INTERNET may appear to fulfil some statutory requirement for contextual studies but the danger is that we become information handlers and information presenters in a global village desk-top publishing enterprise that reduces everything to trivia. Do we travel for the mileage or the culture? An important consideration should always be the intention and the intensity of the search. The only golden rule is that one should buy as much power as one can afford, powerful software on a powerful machine, but then try not to let it lead you into the sort of cunning performance that Master Chuang warns us about. Great art, like great scientific theory, has an inherent simplicity and economy of means. There will always be a place for the slow contemplative evolution of pictorial ideas.

Tony's combination work of text and images enabled us to fulfil our commitment to the National Council for Educational Technology Multimedia and Basic Skills project, securing £2000 funding for the art department.

DEVIL
by Tony Jukes
(Thurlow Park School)
standard page 320 x
256 pixels

FAMILY

by Tony Jukes (Thurlow Park School)

extended page 640 x 462 pixels

Right: preliminaries for **FAMILY**

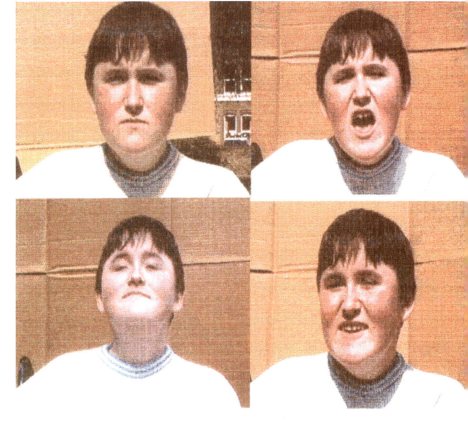

Georgina

Georgina[23] joined the GCSE group with Tony in September 1993. She had always demonstrated an intelligent, thoughtful and competitive approach to any set task, and so consequently had always shown promise of great achievement. But it was the Photofusion project and subsequent self-exploration using digitised imagery that enabled her work to fulfil this promise.

The posters are the only works of Georgina's reproduced out of sequence. **BREAK IT YOU DIE INSIDE** came after **MASK** and **MASKED**. The 'message' of the poster being that art embodies values[24] it being our values that make us human. If we thoughtlessly destroy our cultural heritage because we have no sense of human values then we lessen our humanity. Without values we are soulless, and to be soulless we are as good as dead.

BE HEALTHY BE HAPPY

by Georgina Fitch (Thurlow Park School) extended page 464 x 600 pixels competition poster

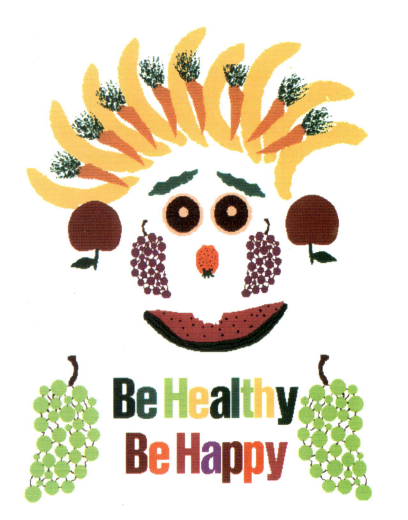

BE HEALTHY BE HAPPY and Tony's **FRY UP** were both created for the same competition. Unfortunately our PaintJet printer went on the blink, one of the plastic gear wheels had a couple of teeth stripped, so we were unable to meet the competition deadline. A pity but then these two have won so much that it was about time someone else got a chance.

Having chosen her gargoyle, Georgina did a simple cut and paste job between the two images, giving herself a lion mask over her own eyes and nose. This worked so well as a graphic image on screen and as a final print that we decided to take it further.

The lion mask was printed out separately and large enough to make a real paper mask which she then held up to her face. We again digitised her image through the video camera, with an unexpectedly beautiful and original result.

Georgina then sculpted the mask in clay, building the clay directly on top of the print, after which the clay was used for vacuum forming in plastic.

Georgina also produced a beautifully mysterious animated sequence with her own image dematerialising and rematerialising behind a mask that slides and falls away. This was probably only her second attempt at animation. (She created her first animation, a snowscene, some years earlier when she was relatively new to the program.) She finished it by the end of the session and needed to get moving so I saved it for her, but I was too hasty and saved it through the picture menu instead of through the animation menu, which meant that only one frame was saved instead of the complete sequence. The following week, when we came to load the animation, I realised my mistake. I apologised for being so incompetent but Georgina

Opposite:

BREAK IT YOU DIE INSIDE

by Georgina Fitch (Thurlow Park School) extended page 320 x 450 pixels
HIGHLY COMMENDED poster for competition YOUR PAST OUR FUTURE organised by the Accademia Italia

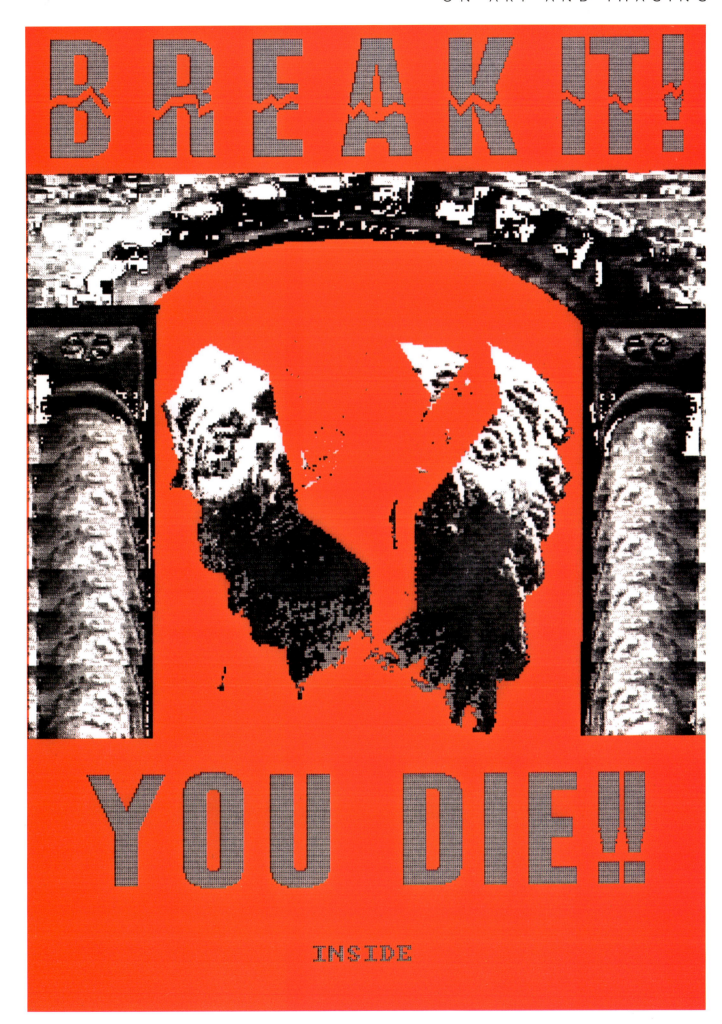

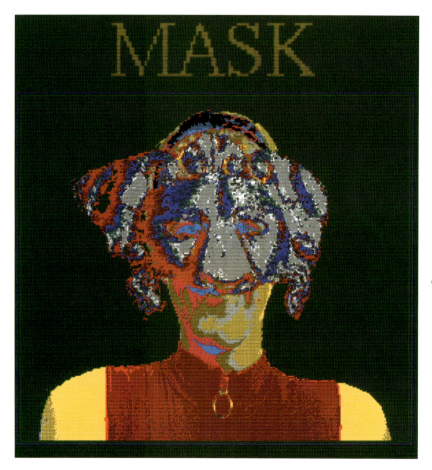

MASK

by Georgina Fitch
(Thurlow Park School)
extended page 320 x
440 pixels

Top right: stone carving
digitised by Jason Lyne

Below right: the mask
as used by Georgina
printed as a cut-out

replied that it did not matter, she would do it again, only better. Which she did. That is another thing I have seen time and again. Students become so confident of their own ability, having learned with the safety net, that they finally no longer require it. Which is of course how it should be. Similar imagery was printed on transparencies, the face and mask separate, and the transparencies mounted as the spatial divisions in a perspex box. When we look directly into the face we see the mask. By moving round the boxed images, the face is unmasked but is then seen in perspective, distorted, dematerialised. This was not as successful as we had anticipated. The transparency film has a slight translucency which is of course cumulative with each successive layer, so instead of the images overlapping clear and bright, they tend to become obscured as though seen through a fog. We may yet find a way round this with clearer film but the animation will remain by far the more effective of the two techniques.

MASKED GEORGINA

Georgina digitised holding the cut-out lion mask

MOON

by Georgina Fitch

print made three-
dimensional by
layering with
lightweight
foamboard
(9 inches diameter)

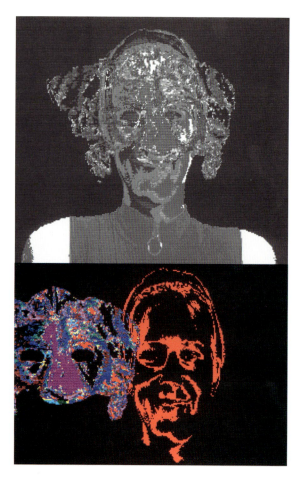

Frames 1, 11, 21 and 37 of 39 frame animation by Georgina Fitch

Georgina continued to develop her work in three dimensions using lightweight foamboard and perspex. **MOON** is a very simple idea but the work has had a strong affect on many people. When moving it or moving oneself slightly before it, the face changes in very unexpected ways.

The various processes which Georgina has used in her work testify to her tenacity, her ability to stay with an idea, allowing it to evolve and developing her practice along with it, stepping from one method to another and from one medium to another, with what we might call the Leonardo da

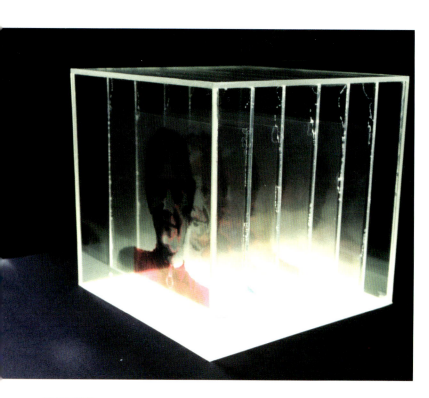

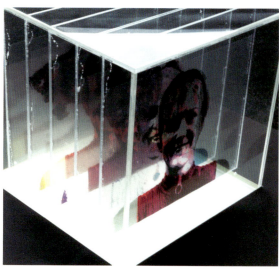

UNMASK ME
by Georgina Fitch (Thurlow Park School)
266mm perspex cube (with thanks to Arthur Elton our workshop technician)

Above: **GEORGINA** scanned photograph

Below: **PUZZLEME** by Georgina Fitch (the same image made thee dimensional with lightweight foamboard 22 x 30 inches including background surround)

FIND ME
by Georgina Fitch
(Thurlow Park School)
the same image as used
for PUZZLE ME again
developed three-
dimensionally with
lightweight foamboard
33 x 23.5 (including
black surround)

Vinci approach or what Feynman calls the chaotic approach: ever experimental, following her own curiosity, allowing the idea to scatter, keeping the response fresh, staying alive. Georgina has been the ideal student for this course. Although there was one slack time when the way became unclear. she was able to acknowledge this and wait until she was able to rise in her own way, producing work of great originality. She paced herself to perfection, exceeding her own past achievements with the final wonderful examination piece, **OPHELIA**. For me, this work is the culmination of the development

Georgina buried in
Ginko leaves. This
image was later used
for her final Ophelia

OPHELIA

by Georgina Fitch
(Thurlow Park School)

The photograph of Georgina buried in Ginkgo leaves was digitised and then printed 22.5 x 34 inches. Georgina shaped the print by cutting the edges and by cutting holes. The shaped print was stuck to a perspex sheet (the surface of the water) 25.5 x 34 inches. Patches of Ginkgo leaves and flower shapes were cut from another large print and these shapes she then cut from thick foamboard using a jigsaw. The flowers were finished with oil pastel and then the thick shapes were added to the 'floating' image.

begun in 1988 with the introduction of computers into art at Thurlow Park: a work based on photography and electronic imaging which finally returns to the processes of fine art.

It is impossible to do justice to this final work in photographs, and therefore perhaps too easy to dismiss it as narcissistic. But ideally we teach in an atmosphere of trust, so engendering self-belief and self-esteem and even, in a sense, love of the self. I value you, you value me, we all value each other

for who we are and for what we have to give, for we give of ourselves. As creative human beings we constantly interrogate ourselves in relation to the world. Jacob Boehme has said that 'man does not perceive the truth but God perceives the truth in man'. In art, and in the evolution of spiritual revelation, and in the revelation of scientific revolution, we mirror nature. By seeing ourselves objectively we objectify the cosmos.[25]

We have demonstrated, I hope, that although using a computer can stimulate creativity by encouraging risk-taking because it gives the artist a feeling of security, it is no quick fix. Just as with conventional art media, where we can gradually build expertise and self-confidence by leading the students through various exercises, so we can give the students time to become familiar with the various possibilities of a painting program. If we refer back to the analogy with word processing, anyone who has written a letter using a word processor will know that what might have taken twenty minutes to write by hand may actually take an hour or more because of the ability to hone the language and perfect the layout. Although at times the computer offers the scope for making global changes, like the well-sweep, it also encourages the pleasure of taking pains, of immersing ourselves in the activity, as the gardener chose to do. In fact that must come first: the steady climb out of the darkness of the well-pit, painstakingly, for its own sake, for love, as a matter of personal integrity. In that sense ethics and aesthetics are one. But there is no short cut to the realisation; only by doing can we know.

Duke Hwan of Khi,
first in his dynasty,
sat under his canopy
reading his philosophy;
and Phien the wheelwright was out in the yard making a wheel. Phien laid aside hammer and chisel, climbed the steps, and said to Duke Hwan, 'May I ask you, Lord, what is this you are reading?'
The Duke said, 'The experts. The authorities.'
And Phien asked, 'Alive or dead?'
'Dead a long time.'

'Then,' said the wheelwright, 'You are reading only the dirt they left behind.'
Then the Duke replied, 'What do you know about it? You are only a wheelwright. You had better give me a good explanation or else you must die.'
The wheelwright said, 'Let us look at the affair from my point of view. When I make wheels, if I go easy, they fall apart. If I am too rough, they do not fit. If I am neither too easy nor too violent they come out right. The work is what I want it to be. You cannot put this into words: You just have to know how it is. I cannot even tell my own son exactly how it is done. And my own son cannot learn it from me. So here I am, seventy years old, still making wheels! The men of old took all they really knew with them to the grave. And so, Lord, what you are reading there is only the dirt they left behind them'.[26]

MOON operating table

Notes

1. My first encounters with computers were negative experiences. Interrogating simple databases and drawing with dreary grey programs was not my idea of fun. I also remember the feeling of utter helplessness and stupidity, my mind benighted and numb, unable to get beyond the *syntax error* message on the monitor screen. The turning point for me came in 1988 when Chris Abbott suggested I look at Paintspa and Art+Time. The bright colour and direct interaction, the possibility of doodles becoming instant animation, were irresistible.

2. Further funding was eventually received from the Peter Minet Trust and the Walcot Educational Foundation

3. Chuang Tzu from **Three Ways of Thought in Ancient China** translated by Arthur Waley, Allen & Unwin, 1953

4. For example ... *The reason I became interested in this field, and can stand here with reasonable lack of embarrassment talking this way about technology, is because of a fluke. I am 54 years old, and happened to be around at the age of seven when the very first loudspeaker was rolled into my classroom, and the phenomenon of BBC radio education was switched on for the very first time. I remember that two things happened: one was an extraordinary amount of interest and excitement among my peers; the other was an incredible level of consternation in the staff room, where the row that broke out was absolutely generational. It was between younger teachers, who saw this as an educational aid and an opportunity, and older teachers, who saw a spectre rolling into the classroom to put them out of work. The latter group assumed that Lord Reith, or someone else in Broadcasting House, was going to dictate the curriculum; that every single person in Britain would be chanting the same mantra, learning the same poem.*

The teaching profession, then, did not embrace technology in 1947; it didn't absolutely reject it, but large sections were terrified of it. And just as all of us now see technology as something we can dip into or dip out of — which is, broadly speaking, helpful to ourselves and to our students — this is the type of adjustment that we are all going to have to make to the new IT. It is out there, it is useful, you don't have to absorb the whole package; but not to pick through it and take the things that help you turn into a better teacher, that enable your students to be better students, is crazy. So please don't let us repeat the arguments, the frustrations and terrors of 50 years ago: let us take a look at this stuff, see how it works and make the best of it. Sir David Puttnam, Culture, Commerce and the Curriculum, NFAE conference report, 1995.

There seems still a great neglect of information technology in fine art courses at both degree and PGCE level.

5. When next we look at an early Italian painting we do well to consider the labour involved, prior to the actual painting, in cutting the panel, sizing, applying glue-soaked linen, applying the layers of gesso, smoothing with a steel scraper, gilding, grinding the colours, etc.. but see **Il Libro dell'Arte** by Cennino d'Andrea Cennini or the National Gallery video: *Art in the Making ITALIAN PAINTING Before 1400*. We do well to remember also the technological changes exploited by the Impressionist painters, such as synthetic colours and mass-produced paint in portable tubes. But see: *Art in the Making IMPRESSIONISM* by David Bomford, Jo Kirby, John Leighton and Ashok Roy.

6. Image processing is a term usually reserved for a program that allows refinement of a given image (in digital form), either from a photograph via a scanner or from a video still.

7. C.G. Jung **Collected Works**, translated from the German by RFC Hull, The Princeton University Press, 1969. **Volume II, Psychology and Religion: East and West, Psychological Commentary on 'The Tibetan Book of the Grest Liberation'**

8. **Chuang Tzu Basic Writings** translated by Burton Watson, Columbia University Press, 1954

9. In his **Notes On Rectangles** (unpublished) the late Patrick S Symons RA writes '*The tension between the picture space and the picture surface, which seems to me an essential element of painting, can be intensified by a greater awareness of the proportions of the surface and possible divisions and points within it...*' It seems to me that this essential tension is something else that is missing when using a painting program, and that we must allow it to *be missing*, although it as it were *snaps back into place* when we eventually see the picture printed.

Patrick often expressed his detestation of computers, but accepted their value in the context of Thurlow Park School, and always found things he liked about the work in exhibitions. After seeing our big exhibition in 1990 he wrote to me from Ryme Intrinseca, '*I am very impressed in ways I had not at all expected . . . the pupils take on such immensely individual and intense work. The porthole full third from the left in Diego's ship seems especially wondrous to me. (The character in the middle porthole upstairs looks very like a pirate!) . . . and the very excited Adam and Eve — How on earth does he think of those particular signs for eyes,*

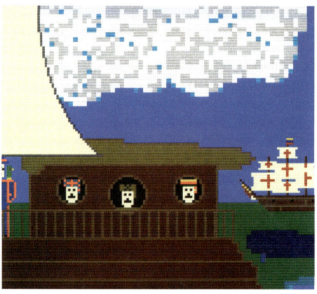

Top: **FNC ARES** by Diego Soto 640 x 512 pixels

Above: The pirates upstairs

Left: The porthole third from left

etc? There is some similarity about the treatment of hair and foam and herbiage which seems a pretty sophisticated try at radiance ...'

10. *'The word 'Hindu', used for convenience, can be misleading, for it may convey the idea that Hinduism belongs to a country, to a particular human group, to a particular time. Hinduism, according to Hindu tradition and belief, is the remnant of a universal store of knowledge which, at one time, was accessible to the whole of mankind. It claims to represent the sum of all that has come to be known to man through his own effort or through revelation from the earliest age of his existence.*

....Hinduism cannot be opposed to any creed, to any prophet, to any incarnation, to any way of realisation, since one of its fundamental principles is to acknowledge them all and many more to come.

Hinduism, or rather the 'eternal religion' (sanätana dharma), as it calls itself, recognises for each age and each country a new form of revelation and for each man, according to his stage of development, a different path of realisation, a different mode of worship, a different morality, different rituals, different gods.

The duty of the man of knowledge, of the realised being, is to teach to a worthy student what he has himself experienced and nothing more. He cannot claim that his is the only truth, because he cannot know what may be true to others. He cannot claim his way to be the only way, for the number of ways leading from the relative to the absolute is infinite. The teacher expounds what he knows and must leave the seeker to make his own discoveries, to find the path of his own development, for which each individual can be responsible finally only to himself.' Alain Daniélou, **The Myths and Gods of India**. Inner Traditions International 1991.

11. Both based on the line drawing of **A HITTITE SPHINX** as it appears in *The Ancient Near East, A Bellerophon Coloring Book*. The Bellorophon books are a superb, and very cheap, resource, presenting ancient and other art in an easily accessible form. They always look to me as though someone has loved selecting all the finest examples of painting and sculpture, presumably as photographs, and then had a lot of fun tracing them and turning them into line drawings. Produced in California, they are available from St Anne's Music Society, 8 Collingham Gardens, London SW9 OHW Phone 0171 373 5566. Catalogue available on request.

12. When I first went to Thurlow Park School, Robert Osborne was in the nursery. We worked together, struggled together, year after year (fourteen years in total), until finally, with the introduction of the computers, he was able, at last, to be truly and independently creative and to take GCSE Art & Design. I have been very fortunate and very privileged to have had the experience of working with him. Robert has been but one of many unforgettable and amazing people at the school.

13. Diego Soto is another remarkable character. His infancy in Columbia and his experiences in this country are detailed in his autobiography **Diego's Story**, Random House.

I taught Diego from the time of his admission to the school in October 1985. I remember clearly our first meeting. I asked him what were his interests and he told me that he liked fast cars and figher aircraft. I asked him to draw either a car or a plane. He drew a car with wings.

His ambition was to be a fighter pilot.

In his spare time, during the lunch hour, he became a regular visitor to the art room. I would give him my undivided attention and he would rapidly 'pace' the room in his electric chair, thinking aloud, flitting from question to question. I answered his questions as best I could. We covered a lot of ground - religion, analytical psychology, philosophy, sex, death, the possibility of an afterlife. Always he would weigh the ideas of others against his own ideas and beliefs, his own experience of the world and people, his own self-exploration.

He even got to be more realistic about his ambition. He knew really that being a fighter pilot was out of the question but he hung on to the idea as a fantasy, one of his many fantasies.

Eventually we acquired the computers for the Art room and I had hopes of entering Diego for the GCSE Art & Design Examination but he became very ill for a while and he chose not to return to the school. He was potentially the ideal computer artist in that he would utilise every facet of the graphics program in order to realise the complex evolution of his multilayered ideas.

His ambition also evolved. He thought he would like to be a genius like Leonardo da Vinci but as he did not really care for the physical effort of putting ideas down on paper he decided that he would rather be a brilliant philosopher like Wittgenstein.

Diego went with us several times to the National Gallery. Michael Cassin, then a lecturer with the museum's educational department, was astonished by Diego's knowledge of classical mythology and Christian iconography and his ability to read pictures. Diego relished these visits as an opportunity to show off to the general public and to convince them that, as he so clearly put it, 'Cripples can think'.

Diego is a thinker, of that there is no doubt.

Since leaving Thurlow Park he has achieved A grades in : O-level Spanish, GCSE English Language, GCSE English Literature, A-level Spanish, and A-level English Literature. He is at present studying A-level Government and Politics and AS-level Philosophy, and he has been accepted by the London School of Economics to begin reading for a degree in Law in September 1996.

14. Ludwig Wittgenstein, **Philosophical Investigations** translated by GEM Anscomhe, Blackwell, 1978.

15. Ludwig Wittgenstein, **Philosophical Investigations**, Blackwell, 1978.

16. Seymour Papert, **The Children's Machine: Rethinking School in the Age of the Computer**. Harvester Wheatsheaf, 1994

17. And not just scientists, '*I slept neither by day nor by night, and forgot both to rest and to eat. Suddenly I was overcome by the Great Doubt. I felt as though freezing in an ice field extending thousands of miles ... It was as if I were out of my mind... It was like the smashing of a layer of ice, or the pulling down of a crystal tower . . . All former doubts were fully dissolved like ice which melted away. With a loud voice I called out, "How glorious, how glorious!" We need no escape from the cycle of life and death, nor need we strive after enlightenment . . . my exaltation welled up like a flood.*' from **A History of Zen Buddhism** by Heinrich Dumoulin, translated from the German by Paul Peachy, Faber & Faber, 1963

In **Zen and the Art of Motorcycle Maintenance**, Robert M. Pirsig uses a supersaturated solution as an analogy for the way the tension of a creative dilemma can lead to a temporary impasse. '*A supersaturated solution is one in which the saturation point, at which no more material will dissolve, has been exceeded. This can occur because the saturation point becomes higher as the temperature of the solution is increased. When you dissolve the material at a high temperature and then cool the solution, the material sometimes doesn't crystallise out because the molecules don't know how. They require schooling to get them started, a seed crystal, or a grain of dust or even a sudden scratch or tap on the surrounding glass.*' The many accounts of eventual breakthrough testify to the continuum of creativity, whether that be the revelation of an artist or mystic or scientist. The result is always a change of *weltanschauung*, whether

Opposite page:

CRUMPET IN THE SKY

by Diego Soto

320 x 475 pixels

The ship in this picture is the FN ARES, picked up as a brush and reduced

that be on a personal or on a global scale. We should remember too that scientists are also guided by aesthetic considerations, that scientific solutions should be elegant, and truth beautiful. But see **Truth and Beauty: Aesthetics and Motivations in Science** by S. Chandrasekhar, University of Chicago Press, 1987

18. Richard Feynman from **No Ordinary Genius** ed Christopher Sykes, Weidenfel & Nicolson, 1994

19. *In the early 1980s there were few microcomputers in schools, but those few were almost all in the classrooms of visionary teachers, most of whom employed them in a 'progressive' spirit, cutting across school's practices of balkanised curriculum and impersonal rote learning Thereafter, however, the pattern changed sharply. The initiative and power in the field of computers were moving from teachers to school administrations — most often at the city or even state level. When there were few computers in the school, the administration was content to leave them in the classrooms of the teachers who showed greatest enthusiasm, and these were generally teachers who were excited about the computer as an instrument of change. But as the numbers grew and computers became something of a status symbol, the administration moved in. From an administrator's point of view, it made more sense to put the computers together in one room — misleadingly named 'computer lab' — under the control of a specialised computer teacher. Now all the children could come together and study computers for an hour a week. By an inexorable logic the next step was to introduce a curriculum for the computer. Thus, little by little the subversive features of the computer were eroded away: instead of cutting across and so challenging the very idea of subject boundaries, the computer now defined a new subject; instead of changing the emphasis from impersonal curriculum to excited live exploration by students, the computer was now used to reinforce School's ways. What had started as a subversive instrument of change was neutralised by the system and converted into an instrument of consolidation.*

This analysis directly contradicts the answer most commonly given by researchers when asked why computers have made so little dent in the problems faced by School. They are inclined to say that 'schools don't know how to use the computer'; and they propose to remedy this by more research on methods of using computers, by developing more software, especially software that will be easier to use, and by setting up channels of dissemination of knowledge about computers. They are fundamentally wrong. Of course, research will increase the variety and effectiveness of uses of computers, but this is not what will change the nature of computer use in schools. The shift from a radically subversive instrument in the classroom to a blunted conservative instrument in the computer lab came neither from a lack of knowledge nor from a lack of software. I explain it by an innate intelligence of School, which acted like any living organism in defending itself against a foreign body. It put into motion an immune reaction whose end result would be to digest and assimilate the intruder. Progressive teachers knew very well how to use the computer for their own ends as an instrument of change; School knew very well how to nip this subversion in the bud. No one in the story acted out of ignorance about computers, although they might have been naive in failing to understand the sociological drama in which they were actors. Seymour Papert, **The Children's Machine Rethinking School in the Age of the Computer,** Harvester Wheatsheaf, 1994

20. Richard Feynman **No Ordinary Genius,** edited by Christopher Sykes, Weidenfeld & Nicolson, 1994

21. James Joyce **Finnegans Wake**, Faber & Faber

22. *Photofusion, 17a Electric Lane, Brixton, London SW9 8LA, provides photographic skills, services and facilities through its photography centre. It seeks to attract members and clients, to provide outreach services to the education and voluntary sectors, and to promote a ladder of educational opportunity through courses, workshops and seminars. Our two-year project was funded by Sir Walter St John's Charitable Trust. Edwina Fitspatrick, artist/photographer, worked with a non-exam group for the second and final year of the project. Geoff Cox, having moved on, did not see the final fruition of all his dedicated work.*

23. Great artist and great athlete, Georgina has competed all over the country wheelchair racing, and has won about thirty gold medals and seven trophies. In 1993 she triumphed in the Seventh National Junior Wheelchair Games in Australia, winning five gold medals for the 100m, 200m, 400m, 800m, and 800m relay, and the silver medal in the all-age Queen of the Track event. She was the first girl home in the 1992 London Mini-Marathon, in which she also raced in 1991,1994, and 1995. And for the past three years in the London Youth Games at Crystal Palace she has held records for 100m and 400m. Truly a golden girl.

24. 6.41: *The sense of the world must lie outside the world. In the world everything is as it is and happens as it does happen. In it there is no value — and if there were it would be of no value.* Ludwig Wittgenstein, **Tractatus LogicoPhilosophicus**, translated by C.K.Ogden, Routledge & Kegan Paul, 1983

25. According to Oscar Wilde:

When Narcissus died, the flowers of the field were desolate and asked the river for some drops of water to weep for him.

'Oh!' answered the river, 'if all my drops of water were tears, I should not have enough to weep for Narcissus myself. I love him.'

'Oh!' replied the flowers of the field, 'How could you not have loved Narcissus? He was beautiful.'

'Was he beautiful?' said the river.

'And who should know better than you? Each day leaning over your bank, he beheld his beauty in your waters.'

'If I loved him,' replied the river, 'it was because, when he leaned over my waters, I saw the reflection of my waters in his eyes.' **Oscar Wilde** by Richard Ellman, Hamish Hamilton, 1987

26. Chuang Tzu. **The Way of Chuang Tzu**, translated by Thomas Merton, Unwin Books, 1970 (Also available in Shambhala Pocket Classics. Shambhala Publications Inc., 1994)

After writing *Pooling Ideas* I discovered **Wandering On The Way, Early Taoist Tales And Parables Of Chuang Tzu**, translated with an introduction and commentary by Victor H. Mair, Bantam Books, 1994. This excellent book also has a glossary of key terms and concepts and is the most complete English version of the Chuang Tzu.

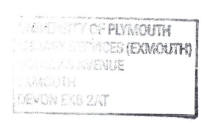